Upon Studying My Exhalation

by Bryson W. Hatfield

DORRANCE
PUBLISHING CO
EST. 1920
PITTSBURGH, PENNSYLVANIA 15238

Dorrance Publishing Co
585 Alpha Drive
Suite 103
Pittsburgh, PA 15238
Visit our website at *www.dorrancebookstore.com*

ISBN: 978-1-4809-3708-6
eISBN: 978-1-4809-3685-0

Contents

Acknowledgments

This is for you, dear reader,

eating up every word with unbroken delight.
This is for you social media clickers,
and cliquers, and "likers" alike;
This is for you sweet, spicy girls,
daring enough to show your bodies but too afraid to care too much.
This is for you, old men,
casting your line out into an endless and
limitless ocean that laps away at your existence.
This is for you lonely, solitary hipster boys,
you that
claim disdain for the universe and still cry at wet kittens;
This is for you fathers out there,
men that spend years slaving for the persistent existence of their
children;
This is for you shattered souls,
and you balanced ones
that don't belong where they breathe in space.
This is for those of you that think that "faggot" is just as bad as "cunt,"
For you that have had to steel yourselves against either of those
slings, time and time again.
This is for you, dear sweet bird,
tweeting your way through
a life in the hot updrafts of the sky;
I know you hear this song.
This is for you thirteen-year-olds chugging slushies at the mall;
for the hundreds of popped kernels, roasted butter and jew fros.
This is for you lipstick lesbians and you lip gloss teeny boppers.
This is for you anxiety-based twenty-somethings,
and you fear-based thirty somethings.

This is for you unpaid actors,
you who bare your soul daily and are truly seen by nobody;
This is for you creatures based from the depths of nowhere,
reaching out to the edges of the universe for what should be inside.
This,
This is for you.

What has been scattered,
though broken and empty in its state of being,
is meant to be collected.
Like the center star in the sheath of Orion,
from a distance, it is soft and glowing,
radiating energy,
but the closer you get, the more you see,
it's all only bits of hydrogen;
the only thing to do,
is breathe it in.

"for The City"

Prayer

One boy in a sea of eight million people just trying to grasp the world.

Noting his own intoxicating addiction to felt tip pens and the way that they resonate across the grit of clean, white paper, he stows his own thoughts in a journal and keeps an open mind, hoping with all of his person that the universe will lose hold of a small morsel of its vast knowledge and that chunk will fall swiftly down to his own mindful orifice, where some moment of truth may be had by him, secretly.

Jay St.-High St.

curled up quiet
don't you move
it keeps the heat in your bones
keeps the warmth inside your coat
keeps the memories of soup in your palms
in your throat your throat your throat

you're rocking stop rocking no more rocking
not like the hero you are no sir no sir no
you have to sit still it keeps the heat
and stop kicking yourself for falling off the tracks
and falling off the tracks tracks
AA doesn't get it
the book doesn't have all the answers

it's hard to see down here
hard to see when you don't even know where you're going
just wait for the lights to pass through
get the flashes every 8 minutes
the flashes of light of truth of some kind of warmth
crawling along the wall

when you get off at Jay Street and walk to High Street
tripping and trippin' the whole way
because something warm through your throat
something burning in your lungs is just what you need
and it's well past six when the kitchen is open
but then it all goes to your head doesn't it
it all goes to your head and you can't fight it away
just blow out the smoke that's all you do
just blow out the smoke with your words that's what you do

words and no one is hearing them
just you and the echoes in this infinite black hallway
doesn't end but somewhere it's deeper
in some places you can get closer to the core
the core of the problem
the core of the earth
it's warmer down there
not so much noise but
the chug-chug
the chug-chug
the chug-chug
that keeps going on so distant and quiet-—like forever
carried on the vibrations of forged steel
and here we are here you are
here put your ear to the wall
hear the ocean
and the pressure in your head it's not so bad as it was
hear the crash of the ocean
and the pressure's not so bad
CRASH crash [hahaha!] crash it away
it's not the ocean it's just a river but it laps like a dog
and it's a saline solution to the wounds
to the cut you got falling off
to the raw callouses that have been eaten off by the rats
saline sweet sweet salty saline to the cuts

you lick your lips they're dry
it's colder the temperature is lower
and you should have grabbed that extra newspaper
more insulation
more heating

a fire would be so good
but the concrete is merciless
merciless doesn't let up doesn't let go
holds on so tight so cold
and it would be better to just sleep
so here it is
the sweet rush of an unbending
muscle falling away until it is only the lapping of the river
echoing hundreds of feet through tired earth and cement
echoing only for you
echoing for your sleeping lullaby
and you drift away with the sound

Specific Width

It appears the strangest thing,
that the sea of eyes being held somewhere
between five and six-and-a-half feet off
of the ground remains the calmest of all
seas in the world.

There is a defiance toward ourselves in
this city. It is a pattern rippling and reciprocating
through the thin fabric that makes up every scarf,
through the small wire that leads up to every white, ergonomic earbud,
through the wax-coated base and milky liquid center of every coffee
cup.
We have seen ourselves dress in the mirror above the sink, and
whether we find it wonderful or not, we still defy the
quintessence of what it stands for, our most basic of human
tendencies to create a connection with another human being.

The current solution: cover your beautiful windows in wax,
wade no deeper in conversation than the shallow pool on your
tongue will reflectively allow you to.

The proposed solution: Clean your windows and show them to
everyone; the soul is a living masterpiece that infinitely captures the
fluid, liquid movement of life and is the central conductor to the
energy that surrounds.
Dive deeply into conversation; this in turn, will never disappoint.

Disbelief and Hypocrisy

I rarely believe a word I say.
In every day conversation, I fear that my mouth will
leak or spew some sort of personal truth. Hardly do I
ever feel comfortable enough to open the valve of
truth that sits in the back of my throat, and share
some form of open communication. I realize that this
is hypocritical of me to say, but here is a
drop of salivated truth
in
the
form of a
drop of ink.

I'm working on it.

Architectural Deficiency

And then it hit me.
Ten floors, hundreds of tons,
all striving for something:
a moment that would sweep them away.

Thousands of people who all only desire the attention.
String, wire, cable, duct work and door knobs
cascade around my mind as the building is torn apart.
The integrity of the structure does not call to me.
It does not instill in my soul, any form of movement;
its contents, however, are precious as the human mind
seems to be.

Weaving back and forth through the halls
does not justify defining walking as an art form in any
case, let alone the one that is contained in the microcosm
of this unfortunately self-aware poem. Nevertheless, those
who weave and wade seamlessly with me have that spark
that could constitute a right to demand such a definition.

I seem to be weaving, myself. Word-weaving and weaving within
and without the collective consciousness that takes place
when a large group of people all have several dozen places
to be at once.

Dozing Thought

Sweet evening sweeps over me.

This wall is a vignette of man-made window coverings and the wondrous rustle leaves of nature, made one by being pressed through a strange, in-between land, into darkness and surrounded by light.

I may or may not draw my own parallels, but who are we to judge?

For the paragon of animals is drawn to simplicity. Even now, things on the outside appear to be simpler, yet the microcosm of their existence is a tumultuous mess of philosophical conundrums and humdumdrums.

The peopled world is the most chaotically beautiful place I have ever laid eyes on.

Elevator Ride

It's your lips, well, that's how it started.
A beautifully curved, dark red streak across the mid of your face,
then your eyes caught me: a rehearsed, nonchalant tweak of the
eyebrows
shows so many people that you care but are too concerned with
other, obviously,
more important things for the time being to do much in the way of,
well…anything about it.

Do you believe we live forever?
In the pages of these books, although we do not
write, does our soul slip in somehow? Hugging the
pole of every exclamation point, sitting cradled
in the soft curve of every question mark.
Do we live forever?

That's what I wanted to ask you today.
I think that, although many people deem it pointless,
dwelling for hours on the concept of immortality is one of my
raisons d'être.
However, I stuck with a single look, a wordless connection into
your wonderful eyes,
warm and inviting though your lids say cruel; my lips,
may just remain sealed like a box with a hook.

Frozen Precipitation

Big fluffy snowflakes falling from the sky,
Quite a different timbre from the Fourth of July.
Double-strong hot chocolate and a peppermint chocolate bark,
Seem to keep my soul warm as the afternoon gets dark.
To top it all off, a Tartuffe-style poem,
Written in A-B for the kids back home.
Now, rock me off to sleep with a harmony so pretty,
All of Broadway dances in my head in good ol' New York City.

A Kind of Sigh

My NYC looms above my head. The city, the people, shiver, and God does what the city asks of it: he lays down a blanket of snow.

The collective exhale of the populace freezes in the air and remains suspended; this morning, you cannot see the tops of the buildings.

I find myself trumping through the blackened purity of winter, wondering when I will cease to feel so alone in a city of so many people.

Each cares immensely about life,
the sanctity, the creation;
living, breathing, caring.

Caressing themselves with the soft chords of their headphone cables; they twang softly against the grit of their clothing, but they will scarcely care to lend two seconds of eye contact…

Writing is treading with rubber boots in the oceanic streets of the Upper West Side.
Each block colors the world around you differently, and discloses secrets about human existence that you
were previously unaware of, intimate secrets.
Here, between 62 and 65 are the secrets of the children that grow up not knowing of mountains,
not caring for the sycamore.
Here, between the library and the green apron coffee shop, is the fountain that is one of the few places where the sound of the city is drowned out in crashing waves of purified chlorine water. They come here to see the star and meditate on life.

Here, between my left ear and my right ear, is the sound of a metaphorical typewriter tapping away in a room filled with stacks of paper piled 'pon filing cabinets.
Some days the keys grow cold; others, they must be wiped clean of the glistening sweat that adorns them.

Today, just like the remainder of the city, I breathed out my sigh to allow a frozen cloud of relief and stress and lack of control to ascend to the tops of the buildings.
Let the cloud be a reminder to the CEO, that the world is not a simple cold, dead place.

Suicidal Hypocrisy

The arguably good artists that cling to our hearts like the last bits of nostalgic Elmer's glue to old construction paper projects have all been snuffed out...

Actually, no.
Strike that.

Take the razor blade edge of the
No. 2 HB chipped-paint yellow pencil and decapitate that thought from the shoulders of the page.

It really has only a margin of the intensity and value with which it originally seemed to possess.

The truism that needs to be expressed here is that in the reality that can only be perceived through one single moment in time

And in no way will be validated now...

Or now...

Or even now...
That moment believed that it was sad that the "tortured artists" of past generations began getting their fixes on cocaine and heroin and ended getting their fixes with taught ropes around the neck and a mouthful of shotgun shell...

That moment felt so much disdain for all of the times that it looked up to these people that were giving him something that he turned into a reason to continue to try toward something more than he was...

In that moment, he hated them for what they did because so much selfishness cannot envelope in just one moment...

One instant is not enough time to justify a premature ending to something that brought life to thousands in fact in makes no DAMN sense.

How hypocritical and selfish of those people. That moment had the weight of the world pressing down on it for a lifetime, and when it finally lifted, it was as if flight were the only answer. Levitation, possible.

But that is not the case with these artists, no.
They fixed themselves physically into the earth through the mediums of long drawn razor blades and stomachs, close to what some might term bursting with sleeping pills,
because our hearts and souls were simply not of enough value.

And how does that feel, dear fourteen-year-old girl listening to Kurt?
Or young man on the subway with that crumpled copy of Earnest?
That your soul being moved by lyrics and movement is not enough to justify life while most of us continue to just breathe regardless of bank account statements or loss of parent...

It seems that the world, to them, was just far too tormented and tormenting.
As dust to the eyes of the young businessman laid to rot in the desert, life dried up all in their sight, and with no water to wash their faces or quench their cracked lips and sticky tongues, they began to see oases in the cool grip of an old shotgun, the bottom of

a new pill bottle, the edge of a razor, and the rough embrace of a solid rope.

And us?

Well, there was nothing we could have done to stop them.

Physical Rebound of Forced Energy

Right now, I'm lying in my bed, and I'm staring up at the creases in the mattress that is suppressing the air above me. I can feel the way that the air is different when I lay down here as opposed to the way that the air is when I am almost anywhere else. It's just not the same to be underneath something so dense and full of interesting, if not pleasant or unpleasant, memories, almost as if the bed itself is neither good nor bad, although a part of me thinks it should be that way.

The fan is on; I always leave it on because if I don't have it on then there is some kind of silence that swoops in to the timbre of the day and ruins all that it touches. The fan simply blows away all of that tension and frustration.

Honestly, I have no idea why you are getting to know all of this stuff... it may or may not have any form of vital application to the world in which you exist now. Just know that I took pleasure and peace in writing this for some strange reason. Let it remind you of the immense humanity that each of us possesses and so many people seem to forget that the other has.

Beginning to an Evening

Take a taste of this; can you handle this?
It's just so "fetch" if you heard that right.

The conflict is talking to that guy,
telling him about myself just a little bit,
becoming more aware recently that
I'm lost, scared, lonely, and stagnant in a city that refuses
to hug me like I want my mother to; love like that can push away
the smog and the stares that drill.

We so often forget the power that two pressed torsos can have,
most of the time even more so than when they lay bare.
In a world obsessed with the carnal and visceral ripping and tearing
and diving and possession and tug-of-war that lies beneath his or
her panting body, we rarely pause for any moment of time to bask
in the beauty that can be had when the innocence of our childhood
comes back into play, and we simply hold one another.

But, life goes on, the glittering diamonds of the cornerstone of each
eye belonging to a lonely stranger sitting on smooth blue plastic;
she is not a part of who I am until I let her emotional reach graze
the tail of my coat. Even then, I do my best to not become a prod-
uct of her problems.

Collar upturned to the feeling as I quicken pace through the guillo-
tine doors, somehow, I'm the same, and genuine emotion used to be
real but now feels counterfeit and stale.

Still, I tread with my green hunter boots away through her puddles;
I will create the objective to absolve myself of guilt as I delve deeply
into the city; you can't feel for everyone right?

We are told how to succeed:
 by finding music in the sound of someone else's name, a love that
sighs on its own accord without provocation, only craving satisfac-
tion when the hours on my wrist begin to yawn, waking up to a late
night text message from the past, from the past.

It is interesting how, when drowning a sea of voices, silence is the
most powerful flotation device. An antidote to the disease of bacter-
ial individuals rubbing past you quickly through the ever closing
evening sky.

Never Ceasing Wonderment

I shoot my life inside the words I want you first and last to know.

Oh Gods, she cried, her mouth outstretched and yawning to the
time-transcendent night sky.
The recoil of tension released,
Reverberated through her chest and down into her knees,
Sharply enough to bend and sit.
What has been referred to as
The "majestic roof fretted with golden fire"
Is mostly empty space... mostly;
There is, however, an acceptable amount of exceptions,
Mostly large clouds of swirling nebulae gas;
If these are her Gods,
It will be a very long time before her voice stirs the hydrogen mole-
cules that make up Their celestial bodies.
When the inevitable reverberation of sound comes thinly back to
her searching soul,
Her body will be wrinkly,
Folded and eroded by the passing waves of time,
And any prayer that is answered will be silently gifted to her
In the still moments of the evening.

As lunar light reflects through the window,
She sleeps and does not hear the young man walk quietly,
Peacefully through the deep silence of the midnight neighborhood.
Each footstep he takes is caring enough to keep from stirring the
Soft down of leaves that create a bed above the cool concrete.

But is it just a good playlist with beautiful souls being established
through the ticking clocks of their own creations?
Or,

Have I finally found something specifically unique in myself,
Vicariously through the looping and progressing and
One two three,
One two three,
One two three,
One two three of the sound?
Has it somehow resonated inside my chest cavity in such a way
That it crafted something entirely new of itself?
Truth be told, I do not know or care to tell if I do.

Enjoying the silence of the night sky is peaceful and wonderful
enough to make me weep.
I find God in the spaces between the white patches.
Like the Lite Brite of my childhood,
Some child in the beginning of the firmament poked holes and bits
of God shone through.
If that is true, then that means that there is more of God between
the stars than there is at the stars.

And I, myself, reside between stars.

Let me take care to not defend one single thought;
Every idea is constantly under attack in my own mind.
Personally, it's as if I have some form of flesh eating bacteria that
has been bred to only attack Thoughts and synapse patterns in my
conscious brain;
I dread to think about how boring I would become if, one day, the
bacteria evolved and began attacking
The subconscious.
For now, it eats only at:
Conscious,

Creative,
Constructive,
And destructive thoughts,
Regurgitating them through a series of chemically imbalanced alterations until they are new.

It would be nice to have such a thing for the soul, don't you think?

Promise: Simply Present

These moments are the most feared,
The ones where the slow stillness creeps up my spine,
Standing with the stale sound of old elevator music in my ears.

"Why are you afraid?"
no.
"Why am I afraid?"
do not.
"Fear is a color not suited for your palette, why are you afraid?"
do not doubt the intimacy of fate.
"Because these are the moments that I am without a doubt certain
that I will be alone for the remainder of my life."
much like the inevitable fate of each text, it has always been written,
and it will continue.

A flash of deep brown eyes is enough to remind that the window of
the soul delves down to the feet, and when we tread, we treat our sole
to what the ground would push into the plastic rubber of our shoes.

Do I scare you? Does it scare you when I think?
No one can ever seem to tell what essence is crushed inside the cogs
of my churning brain.
Truth is, the majority of the time, I seem to scare myself into
thought rather than action.
It's only a fraction of the time that the world around me actually has
reason to be moved physically.

I wish it were as simple as not asking more of these tightly knotted
canvas shoes for more than a continual stepping forward.
More of these hands than soft and subtle, passive gestures.
More of these eyes than truth in the form of visual awareness.

However, the world of excess and deficiency that swirls heterogeneously throughout my synapses demands so much more attention than I am sometimes willing to give it. I don't mean to subtly apologize in my text; it's just that I have a massive fear that one day, inhaling a bowl of sugar-coated corn flakes for breakfast won't hit the spot, and then what will I have?
A stack of papers that adds up to a handful of individuals that will never pay me for the time and energy that I put into what I do?

Let me pour my soul out to you in one brief example:
Traditionally, an artist was commissioned to create some form of art. The marble would be cut, and he would bring it to his place of work. There, he would craft a piece of artwork, slowly shaping the marble into a figure; however, the wonderful part about any form of art is that the soul permanently bridges a gap between the creator (be he a sculptor, a painter, a writer, etc.) and the observer or the imbiber of that particular art through the means of the artwork itself. This is one of the wonderful phenomena that take place in creation. Timeless pieces may be gazed on and when they are truly soaked in through the eyes or any other respective part of the body, the person participating in the art can feel the moment of the artist's soul as if it were in the room with them, right then, in that moment, dancing liquid through the space and enveloping every willing individual with its passionate message.

This, dearest reader, dear beautiful listener, I give freely to you, and I urge you please, take it while you can because one day it may not be free. However, until that day, I promise that I will work as hard as I can to show you every fold and crease that makes up the three dimensional, silky fractal pattern of my soul, and I will pray that you will continue to look, no matter how ugly and honest it may be.

Spreading

Before this,
I never thought that I would feel this feeling about someone again,
That jealousy could be made manifest in the trenches of my heart
Where blood was caught, heated by surprise and hatred at the
words that it was slapped with.
Viscerally, I do not squirm around others, but somehow your
Secret,
Buzzed,
Slight-drunken playfulness has awoken in me a feeling that I had
since forgotten.

That the world should not be a still and lonely place,
That the earth is not cold and dead but warm and alive with touch
and feeling,
That eccentricity of the spirit, the kind that I see in you all of the
time, is good and beautiful, especially when it is allowed to be
drawn to the tangible world.

This I found silently inside myself as your lips feathered over my
overly conscious neck.
It was not a clicking, as a heart opening.
It was not a cracking, as an epiphany occurring.
It was not a crashing, as an entire conscious wall, crumbling.
It was something else entirely:
A kind of spreading,
Spreading as ink over a printing screen, only I soaked it all in.
Soaked in my own emotional response,
My surprise as to what was happening,
Happening, happening, my neck alight with an electricity that I had
not known for a very long time,
your lips.

Oh, the power that lips possess, a hundred thousand words expressed in the pressing of two pair of them together,
Maybe that's why we so often film it.

Let me reach out to steady my own mind because right now, it is tumbling through space at a rate that I cannot understand.
That so small of an action can set such a world in motion and uncertainty of feeling is a scary thing,
So take my hand,
Love,
Knot your fingers and mine together in blue yarn,
Then hold me close, and together,
We'll slow time.

Fact:

Fact 1: I am nearly six feet tall, average height for a guy whose mind daily explodes into a speckled spiral of grey matter.

Associative Fact: Because of this previous fact, I politely require all of my friends to wear safety goggles while around me so no bits of skull catch in their cornea; I do my best to think about others.

Observation 1: I have become quite good at scooping up slimy chunks of thought and throwing them out of my window. It's sad, yet true that the bum that sleeps outside of my apartment gets a piece of my mind every day.

Truth 1: One day, he knocked on my apartment door and gave me back a bit of grey matter that I had thrown out the day previously, "You'll want to keep this," he said to me, a smile parting his greased lips to unveil twisted teeth and blackened gums.
I smiled, took the grimy piece of my own being, mumbled a quick thanks and locked my door.

Observation 2: In my room that evening, I rehydrated the bit of matter with a solution and stuck it under a microscope, only to find that it held all of the birthdays I had ever taken the energy to memorize.
"That's what Facebook is for."
I threw out the bit of my mind.
Consequence 1: I spent the rest of my life bent over a two by three screen in search of the information that was previously available to me at no charge for hourly data.

Truth 2: Knock followed knock followed knock,
Is today important? You forget to remember anymore. It's like a bi-nary code of numbers, but we're all here trying to settle the score of

individuals who seem to know more than we do.

Two weeks ago I lost all of their names,

Last week it was the cities, states, countries.

Specificity is something that does not linger in my mind for long,

with nothing to cling to, the thoughts slip through the Swiss cheese
holes in my brain,

down through each vertebra slowly,

out through my belly button.

Fact 2: Since I started throwing away so much of my own mind, the
explosions have begun to abate. As of now, there is only a mild leak.
However, I sit in my stagnant corner and await the day that the
garbage man will come back with that beautiful grey goop, all of it
collected tenderly in a black garbage bag, and say:

"Your brain really is beautiful, y'know that? It really is. The only
reason it took me this long is because," he will shamefully scuff the
floor at this pause,

"Well, I was busy looking through it,

Sifting if you will."

And I will smile and lean against the door, grabbing the plastic bag
by the tightly drawn double knot and say:

"Thanks, I guess I'd forgotten."

It's Always a Different Fish

We must find the beauty in every evening,
The still stream undisturbed until
The moon sliver orbits its silver into the night sky,
Splashing through, as alive as laughter, this scaled beast,
Up from the meditative gurgle, fishing for flies or lightning bugs.

Elusive, it is only known to the stream by sound,
A swift rush before the slap of the splash
Brought upon the creature by the cruel clutches of gravity.
Flight may never be reached in the world of
Oxygen and
Carbon and
Argon; however,
In a slightly more dense, hydrogenated world,
This spirit flies and rushes through space in any which way.

Knowing a freedom that I only dream of when the clutches of sleep
have grabbed my soul and carried it to a place that is as dense as my
own spirit.
There, I too may float, chasse,
Release myself in fluidity of the space between life and death.

Cave

I wonder at what point I began to lose that youthful quickened energy,
That rapid rabbit paw thump of my second decade, slowly fading to
a sad and lonely deadened clap in an empty auditorium of damned
performers,
Whose nooses tighten as the clocks of their own animal loved ones
tick ever faster onward toward oblivion.

When and how did this come to be?
It is something that sneaks up as silently
As the final exhale one gives before sleep,
You really have to be listening for it,
A whisper whose secret you can keep.

There is no moment of clicking realization that suddenly everything
is completely separate from how it was,
Simply a cold creeping suspicion that the universe has molded you
somehow into a cold, calm, collected being,
Rolled you into a ball, a long thin string,
Tied you into the shape of what you used to be, how you used to re-
main whole and natural and now feel thin and fragile in your own
endeavors.

However, this feeling never lasts for long,
As soon as you,
And of course, by you, I mean I,
Have felt the feeling long enough to put words to it, the feeling dissi-
pates like a very dry red wine, leaving your whole body with an inward
sucking feeling as if it left the world from somewhere inside of you.

I wonder at what point I will feel quenched once again,
Not quenched in the mouth, the tongue, the taste buds,

Quenched somewhere far down in the empty space that resides be-
tween my two rib cages. Where there is
space,
There is a place for the desert dryness to swirl.

It's the lungs mostly; they get the brunt of the abuse. The vacuum
of leaving steals the vapor from their oxygen, and they prune and
dry.

Breathing is difficult, and I crave the theory of drowning from time
to time.
However, some things are better simply theorized… and as long as
confessions are taking place, I'm afraid of fish.

There is, thankfully, a progression of the feeling as time ravages the
planets stone by stone, Molecule by molecule,
It becomes a small light of inspiration.
I can grab it, chop it up, and cook it in my morning eggs so that
sunny side up has a new meaning.

Seasoned with salt and pepper, this small prescription will give some
kind of shielding to the next blow of the vacuum in my chest.

Maybe this time I won't cave in.
Maybe this time I won't cave in.
Maybe this time I won't cave in.

To "An Adoring Fan"

Good sir, I bare not the words upon my tongue to utter the things
that my heart doth feel.
There upon the youthful skyline, the horizon of jagged teeth,
Bukowski wants nothing but to swallow me whole in a world of mi-
sogyny and feminism,
the sky blackening with each vicious gulp of deep red wine.

You, my dear friend, pull me out of the enclosing moment as a trac-
tor beam skylight.
Moonlit path of uplifting ideals with just a single phrase, stopped
time,
to remind me that appreciation is more than what they teach on
Sesame Street as a noun.
You embody the very verbalization of appreciation, and for that, I
want you to know that your soul has
somehow been forever tied to mine.

I recall simply that night we sat together, alone, unattended.
pure and simple.

We spoke of politics, the past,
You said our country needed to know that we only have the tools for
creating what it is that we want out of this stolen ground, that a
great man with a respect for turkeys once said that we had a repub-
lic "if we can keep it."
I said, "I've always been one to keep things that ought to be let go:
old plastic bottle caps, the chewed up remains of my pen tops, girl-
friends. So maybe I'm not the best person to decide if things are ac-
tually worth keeping around, if I'm worth keeping around."

We spoke of science, the present.

You told me that the universe, in all of its infinite space, at one point began at a singularity. You told me that you believed in the traditional Newtonian ideal that "if I see further, it's because I'm standing on the backs of giants."

I retorted that I simply see what is around me and I wonder when the giants will become the earth, when the buildings that cut through the jet streams of cloud will become the floor underneath my feet, and the stars will be at eye level.

You sipped your tea.
Your hands always shake; why do they shake? Too much compassion bubbling at the tips of your fingers, I am ventured to guess.

We spoke of love, the future.
Our silent conversation rippled through the room, rustling old pages and your soul and mine smiled in unison,
like two old souls do.
You said that you loved her; I congratulated you, voices and souls such as yours do not find compatible matches in the likeliest of places.
I told you I feared love, love in all its hurtful disdain.
You said that it's always worth it to go through an inevitable pain for a moment where two people can
share something more than conversation and physical ease.

I said, "I have an idea."
We took our texts and shredded them, dissertations to pieces, adding water and paste we mixed the words together, working the text into a moldable clay, we coated
our feet with the thick paste and pressed them together holding them firmly until our soles hardened

together and you smiled, our process complete,
we both said in unison:
"love is what defines us."

Pinprick: A Lament

I need a golden thread of threnody to draw through the eye of a
pinpoint needle;
Silky smooth, it caresses the curl of metal and is drawn through
with the soft ticking song of friction.
My threnodic thread, pure and clean as new fallen rain, is
Innocent as a child's cough in a hushed classroom during the sepia
era of apples on desks.
For this thread, once fed through the needle's eye, can begin to
serve a medicative purpose.
I am a man with a chest cavern open to the world.
People may see my heart and brush it with their eyes and their in-
fested hands of need,
So this needle with the wonderful woven thread can do something
wonderful indeed.
With it, I can sew the cage of my heart together, piece by broken
piece.
With it, I can reassemble the world that was once ordered organi-
cally, to have a resting place for my
lungs at least.

Window

It never does cease to amaze me,
The amount of dislocation between two human beings standing
only fractions away from one another.
It is a lesson that intimacy is something not measured by particles
that span the gap between two entities.
Whether dozens
or billions,
The amount of particles does not determine the intimacy at all.

Truthfully, I feel more intimate with the man who is sleeping on the
passing subway across from me. Our cars each came to rest at a similar speed for a brief moment before his express sped off, but for a
snapping instant I saw him and he saw me.

He was relaxed up against the railing, a seasoned veteran, unencumbered with the weight of the city, a man who did not deem his
world to be as flashing and dangerous. He leaned quietly, head
cocked, a listener of the world.

What he saw in me I can only venture to guess was a man who drew
strength from pursed lips but melted like a wax candle at the beauty
of a shared moment between two souls who knew that there were
better places than these.

For this reason, our particle count was none.

Amid the Rats

Glances into the trough of the subway system,
As it lays barren and devoid of its humming crunch of electric brake
on smooth smothered rail, Reveals a secret.

Each discarded bottle of liquor and dropped can,
A still life testimony to the weariness that pervades the lungs of each
breathing man.

Where does the essence fling to when inevitability comes barreling
down the tracks?

End of Day

Seldom do we take time,
Exhale the day,
Treat the soul to serenity
That gift ending of the day's labor,
Introversion, found within a rainbow,
Now seconds of painted paradise
Glimmer, shimmer, for a moment, in my eyes.

Reverb

Reverberating, the sweet whispering wind from the subway, echoes behind its missile.
A rotted banana, old hobo vomit kind of tint carried on its breath.
The vomit is old, not the hobo himself.
This moment strangely is a reminder of days when the world was silent around me.

Days when a beautiful blue kayak rested on a lake that was glass, and the silence of birch and ancient oak dampened the thoughts of car horns and specific latte orders.

Days that were two hundred pages lost in a book; lost in a world unlike any known before, free for twelve hours before the ticking or drip dropping of a Chinese water torture day was made to resume...

These days hold some kind of silent ebb and flow; the lake that they swirl in is vast as a conversation, ever expanding fluidly like warm oil on a smooth metal surface.

They are golden, valuable as rich soil to crops, as the sun.

They nourish.

I cannot let them go.

To the River on 60th and Broadway

There are things that remind us to be human.
The brush of a cheek against the downy fur of a canine counterpart.
Two souls fighting to keep their love in a city that forgets.
A small boy standing on the edge of comprehension,
Hands in pockets,
His eyes intently fixed on the bubbling rush of water before him.
The gift of a city: a river down the center of a street.

The sweet intensity of a rushing breeze, something to remind that
you are missed daily.
It's just that some ticking seconds seem to hold their breath till
they ache;
The thought of seeing your face once again is simple as soft puppy
down,
or a whispering accidental river down 60th Street.
So though it feels as if I am constantly being recoated in an
ever-hardening shell for the protection of my own sanity,
I can be eroded by the river of your silent words and find someone
who is more human, simpler, and much happier.

Slow Boom on 72

The slow bloom of the city is showing me a part of itself that I have not known until this day. Taking the time, as I drag slowly on my afternoon coffee,
to take in the humid rain that has been sucked into the air like a mirage into a parched tongue: only the concept of it exists, and as soon as you are attentive of it, it puffs away in a mist of dreamy haze.

Millions of people crowd the exits and entrances;
the labels on the doors are arbitrary because people will go where they need to go because they need to go:
lesson one.

Every ten-minute cycle is a rumbling beneath my feet,
thousands of individuals rushing and running,
and today, I have taken the time to be stagnant
for one singular moment.

That's lesson two: they don't stop moving.
Never.

Fitzgerald called them "waves borne back ceaselessly into the past,"
and he wasn't wrong.
But time has pushed the interest of the waves into a more futuristic direction.
Always needing something more,
always moving forward.
They can never be content with the now,
and they can never be all alright because
there is always a new application to apply, applicably.

Here, sitting, I wonder if I'm the crazy one that's lost it.
Just knowing that because it rained, it reminded me of my shower
two days ago in which I sat on my haunches
and asked my muse where she had gone over and over and over
again.

Because creativity does not come easily to me.
Words do not flow like the ocean of
earbuds and subway trains that I drown in daily, no;
they flow like pulling floss out of a cheap plastic container,
or like pulling a piece of chewed gum off of the seat of your pants.
Words do not come easily unless she's there: my muse.

I guess she took the 3 Train to Harlem.

So today, I'm waiting for her to come back to 72 and share a cup of
coffee with me.

"for Love"

Response:

This goes out to a strong bird,
to a beautiful bird with soft down
and a large poof of feathers atop her head.

She flies all over,
sweeping through the air,
kissing the oxygen with her bird songs,
and she has since begun to build a nest inside my chest.

I have to say that I am surprised that my body is not rejecting
twigs,
grass,
clots of earth,
but I have somehow become immune.

And she nestles so softly right there
where my heart should have been,
where I thought it was.

When she flies south for the winter,
I pack her with shredded letters and
carbon copies of my poems,
Something to chew up and line her nest with on
nights that her down fails her;
I want her to know that I won't.

I get telegraphs from her,
time to time,
short and long ticks of information.

They tell me she's ok,
that she misses me,
that she wishes there was more of me there than just words.

I want her to know that there is,
somehow.

And that there's also a nest in my heart,
unattended.

A Kind of Wish
that Slipped Between the Airwaves

There is so much feeling and pain and celebration in this world. I wish I could show everyone how I see it. It's such a beautiful thing to behold, the balance of the world and how small we are in comparison to everything else that's going on in this vast universe. Out there, among the stars, it's always night time and always day time; it's always the perfect time to love someone, and that energy and time is here now. Some people take advantage of it, and others don't, and whether you do or do not, it doesn't matter because the opportunity will not cease to exist as long as there is air somewhere to breathe. I just wish I could breathe air in close enough proximity to you to push away all thoughts of darkness.

Contextual Analysis

I love you.

He punched each character in with the tips of his thumbs, and at every tap, it was as if a new level of peace had approached him so that once the phrase was written, there was serenity in his grasp, reminding him not only of the solace and comfort that she offered in her careful, lovely words and warm heart and mesmerizing eyes, but also the peace that he himself was capable of creating personally in stressful situations. It bloomed inside him like a small white flower, and its essence filled his stomach until the flavor was in his mouth; there it sat as a floral arrangement upon a pink, mushy table in a room that is scarcely looked at and hardly ever inhabited by other living things, ruminating throughout the night and mixing with his dreams.

When he finally yawned in the morning it puffed out of his mouth and dissipated, cloud-like into the air. The floral essence leaving a sticky sweet aroma above his head. It fell in his hair, and upon pulling his V-neck over his head it rubbed off on the inside of the polyester-cotton mix.

From here, it mixed with his daily perspiration and dried on his skin. Marinating the outer parts of his soul until they were tender with care and compassion. As evening swept around once more, a shower rinsed the excess bits of essence over his body and away from him, but the little bit that stayed was enough. The small amount that soaked through to his soul was enough. Just as she would always be enough and just as he would always wish to be enough for her.

No Reason

it's these times
[these brief moments],
that are strangely the happiest.

not the rushing warmth of the car heater,
juxtaposing the cold [thin] night air,
my hand brushing the stream,
the cooling oxygen turning my fingers slowly colder.
because in those moments, you're the captain,
a black and white etched memory of a mouse
piloting a steamboat down the river.
I'm the smoke in the stacks
[puffing round and deep into the air],
a product of your enthusiasm.

[it's not supposed to be complex.
it's just a simple metaphor
for something complex
[it's a simplification
of a complex thought that I
have over and over on a daily basis],
and I could blame it on my neuroses
but I want to get it just right.]

because from the freshly drawn heart on your hand
[the one beating from my inkwell]
to the heart that you refuse to wear on your sleeve
[the one that I only see pulsing on the surface of your neck],

there is
honesty in your stillness,
beauty in your silence,
peace in the sweetness of your breath.

and it's all that I can do to smile
for what you would see as
no reason at all.

Fishing for a Prayer or a Dream

Scent sense returning through proximity,
it's sweet sweet flavor, sweet aroma
because it's the first time in a long time.
It's been such a long time coming, and now it's here,
and you're here,
and this is an embrace made most sweet by the subtlety of it
but also just sweet of you, kind
in a way. The whispered secrets are enough,
ones that are unspoken,
pressed through the palm of your hand,
pressed into the palm of my hand,
and it's sweaty, I'm sorry, but you say it's human.
I believe it's human.
If it weren't, what would I be?
Something different than what I am would be something unknown
to both of us, I believe,
but it's not that, it's human,
and it forms a sort of slick bond,
and your palm pressing is better than I can spin with words,
and the pads of your fingers, the pads of your fingers,
they're pressing too, and it's like a Morse code,
a beeping and a pressing and my hand is encased.
I'm so safe in this for some reason;
I'm so safe in the wrap of your hand,
in the quiet of your breath.

And I trace on the back of your sleeping shirt
quietly when your breath is slowed to an ocean wave,
and I hear my finger catching on the fibers of the gray,
the gray, the gray cotton shirt like little hooks,
fishing for a prayer or a dream,
in between the time that I sleep,
and the time that sleep takes me.

Minutes

Such a distance I've traveled,
and the rolling sea has carried me,
rocking waves knocking me farther,
distancing me from you,
and now, we are handfuls of minutes apart,
no longer handfuls of inches.
Distance measured in time over rate,
rather than actual units that fit
into the palm of my hand,
units that fit.

Like the small of your back, fit.
Like your soft curving waist, fit.
Like the back of your neck, fit.
Like my fingers in your hair, fit.

And now, it's thin minutes stretching,
melting away with the heat of time.
Distance measured in fractions of an hour;
you're three quarters away from me,
and I wish that wasn't true.
I wish that lips were locked,
fingers laced,
feet were shuffling in a soft waltz,
run on a tune inside my own rhythm.

But you are minutes and not inches
away.

You Had to See This Coming

you must have seen it,
sweeping down the plain.
it cooed like a bird,
taking the shadow of doubt in its beak.

enveloping you in its feathers,
freeing you with its birdsongs,
lifting you high into the air,
only to drop you like a stone.
you silly clam,
you have no power against the crashing waves;
the rocks do not hold back,
and you are cracked, exposed.
the only way out is to find the freedom in the shattered
dimensions of your shell where the light comes in.

only then can you find your peace in pain.

Pale Blue Polyester

Don't inhale,
it's a danger to you.
you won't die, no; I promise
no physical harm.

Deep in this cloth,
there are memories,
broken ideals,
and to breathe them is a drug,
a smell that will grip you around the lungs
and pull you back to quiet nights
spent in company and somehow alone.
But of course, you would never know.

Just hold tight,
hold tight;
sometimes a smell is the deadliest poison,
sometimes the best medicine.

Waves

It's a wave that rushes in,
cresting on the brush of a finger pad
in the midst of a hug.

Reminding of the sweet embrace since sewn,
now decayed,
meant never to reap,
only to be cut off at the root.
No clutching forces available
because the soft underside of arms
has slid away to reveal
a cold calculated and concave
indentation in the frame of the bed.

But it's a wave that rushes in, it
sweeps and smooths the shore,
and sore muscles inside cages that
reverberate their shattered tragedies
(their melodramatic casualties)
can be restored.
In breath and stillness
and the reapplication of loneliness,
the re-appreciation of singularity.

Until –of course– the next wave.

Sticky Hands

My niece at age one,
she developed this disdain
for sticky fingers.
A strange habit, to say the least,
for a twelfth month.

Peanut butter and jelly
became almost impossible.
Pancakes were nearly unthinkable.

Almost immediately, there would need to be
the application of a damp wash cloth,
or a wet wipe,
or a swiftly running sink.

The funny thing is,
I never thought that I would be
the stickiness on your fingers,
and I never thought that
it would be so necessary to clean me
so quickly from your hands.

But the fun part about being
the stickiness of your fingers
is how easily I can tell
it would be for me
to adhere to your pads and palms again.

The kicker is,
you said you're quitting sugar,
and I'm not quite as sweet as I was.

Him: Her:

Him:
Her smell,
and her hands,
and her teeth,
and her feet,
her red hat,
I'm not allowed into that world anymore. Nope.
Locked out, no key.
Set to wander the NASCAR track of my mind,
wandering and wondering what was right,
what wasn't.
It's not healthy, wondering in circles.
It's a disgusting habit;
might as well smoke while you think,
or think while you smoke
(though that's less dangerous),
wander and wonder on, take no shortcuts,
slice no corner too thin,
and tread lightly on eggshell body.

Her:
Her smell.
and her hands,
and her teeth,
and her feet,
her red hat...
It's a matter of perspective.
But beauty stems from the gut;
anyone saying different hasn't seen the root.
But some roots are deeper than others;
some reach through the feet and bloom.

Others stop in the thighs;
others still wither and fade.
But some permeate the entire body,
covering it with individual internal
beauty. This cannot be shaken.

Whatever this is [I want it to be me]

It started here:
"I wrote and wrote and wrote until you were nothing more in my mind than a scar washed clean with a healthy dose of depression."

Whatever this is, I want it to be me right now,
not just you alone.
(Breath)
I hope
that the space in between us is not just taken up with words spoken but things said, that your purposeful licking of lips is not just some subtle intellectual intention for me to read with my screaming head that, when deciphered, tells me that you're somehow ok for me to fall sweating down on that space between your hips,
but no,
we're not easy like that; we're classy. We make due with our words stolen from English classrooms and our clothes stolen from the first tart crunch of original sin, and it's somewhere deep within our soft eyes and sunken cheeks that we forget the very fabric of our culture and strive for something separate.

Whatever this is,
whatever this is,
whatever this is,
I want it to be me.
(Breath)
This right here, standing,
wondering if I'm sinking into the floor
and afraid that I might be because I know that I can't move,
I haven't been able to move like I used to; I'm just getting older.
But I'll pretend like I do, like I am.
I'll pretend, and you'll smile and shake your head,

short poof of hair swaying slightly.
(Breath)
I'm proud to call those moments mine
because whatever they are, I want them to be me.

Whatever this is,
frozen flowers of ideas ripped from the stem.
Whatever this is,
a bombshell dropped on a Gerber daisy.
Whatever this is,
undeserved shouts that wish to be directed at a vast expanse of noth-
ingness because that's where they
belong.
I want it to be me.
I want it to be me because the root remained intact.

I want it to be me because the bomb was only a sketch.
I want it to be me because a true apology is one of the most difficult
things to do.

I wrote and wrote and wrote until I was nothing more in my mind
than a boy washed clean with a healthy dose of depression.

Clean, hopeful, driven, and hoping that, when it comes down to it,
it's me.

Chocolate and Wine

I won't lie, at first I began by pretending to ignore the slight bash-
fulness of the attraction to your subtle freckles, then it could all no
longer be helped.

And everyone seems to think it's in any form of control other than
the form in which it is...
that I'm in any form of control in that state in which I am.

But I pad away desperation with the beat of fresh broken chocolate,
and the soft pop of a bottle of merlot,
and the underlying pacing of my own exhalation,
and then I forget the freckles.
I forget the freckles,
I forget the freckles,
I forget the freckles;
every last angel kiss, something I
could never give, never take away,
it all just fades with chocolate and wine.

Sharing

My love,
he told me that you were electric,
that it would be wise to stay away,
and that there is a strange toxicity to you lips.
I can't resist it.

Sorry to say that each bite brought blood
to the surface of your skin,
each hickey,
and damn me for breaking the porcelain lining of you.

He said to give it time on my own
to better itself and
float through time ethereal; however,
I'm not one to listen too intently,
and he's not one to give up on a woman
that yanked his soul from him somewhere back in '96.

So we share softly and gently,
easily and swiftly,
through man-made ideals
like liquid and lavender oil,
and that is how we suspend
disbelief in one another's similarities
and faith in one another's differences,
trekking and ticking our way through life.

Recreating Heaven

Two lost wandering souls circling,
too comfortable for small talk,
and without divine intervention
to push them closer toward the future,
they fill their mouths with stars,
with space and ocean and the secrets of old dust,
with the exhalation in an old rocking chair and baby's breath,
found on nights where the only acceptable sound is the river that runs
through the back of the property,
and these two lost souls get the feeling that they know it,
they know these woods,
they know the komorebi in the trees by the orange and pink of a sunset,
these secrets are fulfilled in the molars behind their teeth and they kiss
and their bubblegum breath is sweet.

She says, "If I were to recreate heaven, it would be this sound and this
light. Peacefully falling through images of rushing water, waving
grass, the smell of sweet wheat, and the warm smell of sunshine."

He says, "If I were to recreate heaven, it would be this sound. A blur
of the texture of brass doorknobs, worn wooden floorboards, the af-
termath of the silence of a storm, you know, that smell that happens."

Two lost wandering souls circling
amber light from the corner, coloring the scene sepia,
and it's all
slow,
pushing
through
tree sap
as thousands of times before,

knowing young trees to expand to old oaks between lifetimes,
between blinks,
feeling the quiet hush of each breath,
the electric waves emanating from the pads of the fingers,
noting how they give and take equal
parts of energy in every minute long second;
the small string of saliva connecting two pairs of lips,
so strangely human and yet so not,
suspending both of them between the surface of the earth and the
gravitational pull of its nearest satellite,
slowly twisting in the atmosphere,
feeling the ozone kissing the pores on their skin.

She says, "You're so cute, you're so cute, you're so cute."

He says, "I will let you love me for as long as you like, and I will love
you for as long as you let me."

To an Infinite Girl

My dear hardly finite girl weaving through my thoughts,
I would try to write something beautiful for you, but it would be one
of many, much better pieces Written
Without me,
But I'm trying to, just the same,
To prove that you stand on your own breathtaking springboard,
So infinitely close to the sky, swearing that you can reach the stars
pulsing in your uneven irises,
And so aware of this halo around us, circling and encompassing our
thoughts and energies, Gazing out
Over the oldest city in the United States, feeling the timelessness of
each shared flitting second.
And becoming somehow intertwined,
Like the fabrics in your cute hat,
Like my newly ringless fingers,
Like my heart with yours,
All of those being somehow as finite as the stars and nebulas burning
apart over time.

Siren: You (Past Lives)

I wonder that I was a man of the ocean so long ago,
tanned like leather, sweat salty in my eyes,
feet bare and splintered against the deck of my home in liquid chaos,
I wonder that I was: a man knowledgeable of knots, more than capable
of high climbing the mast,
void of vitamin c, body slowly wrecked from scurvy.

And I wonder that you were a siren,
a woman of water,
hair flowing and chucking and tossing in the sea foam and the kelp,
and you picked me from the ship as a ripe cherry,
you drowned me in your intoxicating songs and filled my lungs with
salt water,
I fell in love with your gills
and the mucus between your webbed fingers,
and as my light began to asphyxiate
like a lidded candle, I knew that it was meant to be.

Wondering at it now, I hope it's true
that you were the death of me in love
long ago, past time and bodies,
because now it's equal, and love cannot kill me.

A Thimble, Ma'am

It starts with the electric shock in the mouth,
a small burst of what's inside her eyes,
and it flows through the teeth,
copper and steel flavor
down the throat,
igniting the fire in his gut
through the thighs
down to the souls, the soles,
of his feet,
grounding him in a way that he didn't know before.

And timeless hands
entwine in teal yarn,
and old souls press closer,
remembering times spent beneath
an old willow with wine and tales,
a president's birthday,
a freshly published book,
all of them together there in that moment.

Gradually, lips press,
and the future explodes,
catches on fire
behind softly resting lids,
and breath is one and nothing,
within and without it all,
weaving between dream sequences
where the two collided in stardust,
creating nebulas in their explosions
where the two crossed as soft clouds,
passing through as water vapor through the atmosphere

where they just missed one another,
clipping the wax fixed wings of their escape of life, sending them
spiraling to the maw of the ocean. and
then lips part,
yanking thousands of shuffled
years away from one another;
two half-decks of cards complete in their unity,
individual in their separation,
keeping in mind the secret that each of them has tucked away,
that they belong just less than everywhere and just more than
nowhere simultaneously,
and anything less is only a kiss.

"for Knowledge"

Half-Life

What is it then?
What is the space between us but ancient air,
crumbling, degrading, burning away with time?
In years, we may still be physically as far apart,
but the distance between us merely a few inches;
or,
due to my own lack of knowledge in particle physics,
that time could be now. The half-life of space is
rarely calculable on an emotional level.

Vernacular Injustice

Infrequent moments pass,
When cinematography shows it's true
insincerity, that the real moments,
the poignant times that you wish you had six cameras capturing at
once,
staring at a light infested ceiling,
wishing for some kind of purple truth
that loves you like old worn sheets.
Sitting half-drunk, listening to the
timbre of someone else's soul in c-major,
scaling backward through time as
the universe slowly unravels its lonely
truth, you fight to keep the tears at bay.
Some things in this world mean more than a thank you can suffice
and even if it
did, there would be injustice among
vernacular.

Nathan: An Epitome of Creation

Man step me once,
Tuck him down mid word,
Tackled 'm and felt somethin' crack,
Mighta been 'is chest.

But I slammed him a good one,
No man tha' knows me gon'
Try'an step me like this one did.
Not 'ny more 'nyway.

I pin't him good and beat him,
Whole crowd started gath'rin, tellin' me
T'stop.
But I didn't. I jus' kep' on slammin'
My fists into his chest, his face, his neck,
Lookin' ta bring some part of me that was in him out.

I was like a fuckin' sculptor,
Feelin' his bones 'n skin 'n blood 'n
All kinda, whatsit, congeal together,
Or somethin'.

I sculpted him ta what he was when he spoke: a dead man.
Then when he was finished, I stepped back and raised my hands, my
brushes, right?
Cuz I'd made somethin' that had enough of me in it for people to
know who I am.
An' that's art, ain't it?

An Evening Flash

I can close my eyes on certain days
when the night is calm,
when the stars glow softly
on the landscape of someone else's ownership.
I can close my eyes and see lightning arc across my retinas.

It's neurological,
an adjective
of or relating to the anatomy,
functions
and organic disorders
of nerves and the nervous system.

But it's beautiful,
something secret, like the ticking
zen hands of my grandfather's watch,
Speidel express,
water resistant.
It says quartz,
but those details are unimportant;
what it does is tick,
which
to a loud and disorganized mind
creates some kind of order,
as if counting the moments toward
an oblivion in which we will shake hands,
an ethereal moment where he'll look at me and say,
"Nice watch, young man."

And lightning will arc across my retinas as now,
reminding me of uncontrollable tremors,

moments that have shaken my body into a cluster of bruises,
my legs, old bananas,
my tongue a rare steak.
But somehow these evening flashes are peaceful,
euphoric almost,
as if they are leaving for good instead of crossing
the iris.

If only that were possible…

Water

Liquid in motion, traversing the curve of my arm,
gravity pulls as a child on his mother's hand, constant and innocent.

Liquid in motion, warming angel kisses on my shoulders,
Mom used to call them; she said they were just stains from the lips
of heaven.

Liquid in motion, down the back of that gym class statistician;
Dr. McCarthy deemed lacking in misalignment enough so that I
was allowed to play badminton with the
other kids.
I didn't know back then, but some classmates weren't so lucky;
they flipped a different birdie toward a classmate and said she had a
back shaped like a lightning bolt.
As if she was the only person who had electricity and rage running
through her spine.
Daily, unbeknownst to me, my spine was misaligned in an invisible
way, irregular synapses misfiring in
my brain.
Don't tell me it doesn't feel different when you wake up on the floor
of a boys' locker room shower,
dripping with soap and praying that you'll remember your name be-
fore next period,
thinking "Oh my God, I hope no one saw that."
Liquid in motion, a hard water stained shower head museum and
the strange feeling that any of us actually belong to a similar
species. Staring eyes are the most feared sight for a half-naked, thir-
teen-year-old epileptic.

Liquid in motion,
feeling alien, slimy and wet. Might as well take your time now; go
through the check list.

Head: Nothing broken or fractured, just the glasses and dignity.
Tongue got out of the way quickly enough.
Remembering the name is always the hardest at first, then the
birthday, what is my birthday?

Torso: Should be just fine. Abs are always sore afterward, and the
lungs hurt, but that's just a muscle.

Legs and below: if I peed, no one noticed, thank God for that.

Liquid in motion, warming angel kisses on my shoulders,
there's a bruise in a blank patch, but they'll kiss it better.

Morpheme

Do you feel the magnet power of attraction,
that permanent gravity aching that squeezes us just
a little tighter than we were?
We communicate it so differently to one another.
Some days I'm speaking a mix between Latin and ludicrous, and
your
Spanglish cross Italian pings off of the wall of my chest,
only some words and emotions sink in through the skin,
oils that nourish the soul deeper than a kiss on the cheek.

It's better, it's a kiss on each palm with lips of acrylic paint,
paint brush, rabbit fur soft, caress the calluses.
Even the rough hands of day labor need to be reminded that love
is more than moisture on the skin, it's wishing well deep,
echoing back with the ping of a dropped coin,
the reverberation of a life spent as a singular soul with a wish and a
coin.
Frustrating to realize that the cold, grey rocks that walled off the
deep kept out more than unwanted bugs, kept out dreams,
kept out the magic to grant wishes.

My hands, you covered with soft pressed lips,
and it was better than any pain killer I could have taken.
You said that love was the most powerful word ever spoken;
I retorted that in the world of linguistics,
the word love fit into the category of the more unproductive mor-
phemes
alongside
cat,
poop,
ouch.

Therefore, it had some form of fatal flaw that could be exploited just like me.

I don't know why I said that,
I thought you'd laugh, but your face dropped, and you just asked me how long I'd known.

Your coat was a chaos of tightly woven thread that you threw around your arms before you walked out of my life.

First Taste

Cup resting on lips,
a soft, gentle caress, past
the bilabial region butter and spices.

Hand swirls 'round the glass,
grinding sounds beneath the red,
conversation sparks madness,
quiet in the brain.

Poem

Even sloping ramps that guide,

Point A: beginning an ascent from
zero ground of understanding,

Point C: arriving at an
ultimate understanding,
the first step on a separate level,

Point B: transitional phases,
the most imperative of the points,
human moments that survive,
immortalized forever.

Small breaths,
each catch holding within itself,
a microcosm of the world,
these more important than each bullet.

Old Picture of My Grandfather

Thumb to pointer finger, chin height,
Arm extending through the ages,
The sharp dressed man reciprocating
The flash of the camera to me now,
It is reflected in the twinkle of his eye.

His boyish demeanor emanating from the casual
Sweep of his hand to his pocket,
The soft creases that originate from there,
The slight tip of his hat,
Balanced by his genetically large ears.
A beautiful sight of a man,
Although his stories are now told silently,
Spinning for hours, his tales, and yet still,
Finding their correct time and place in the mind.

"You are what you do."
"You are what you do."
"You are what you do."

I salute you, colonel, and although I'm ill equipped,
I still beg the question, what does that make me?
And more, what does that make any of you?

Theatre: A Definition

If A performs B for C then…

1) B does not have to be anything specifically creative,
   Nor does B have to be a text or a poem or anything written.

2) B indefinitely approaches infinity.

3) A and C are both in the same space and should be at least
   semi-cognizant.

If these stipulations are met, then theatre is present;
however, art may not be.

Flies

Fingers rubbing against the cold,
she walks through the doors of the
bold-type, name brand coffee shop.
Each visit is equally as unannounced
as the next and the previous,
and the barista finds her to be
just as bothersome every time.
"Something sweet."

"$5.59."
Pocket change rattling on faux marble top,
temporary relief is sucked down the gullet
through a sickly green straw.

His fingers tick softly against the touch
pad of a mass marketed tablet, the caramel
residue leaving small prints on the letters
past, present, and possibly future.
He sits in his false, scrap-metal chair and lets
the world spin around him, trailing a light beam
around the circumference of the earth.

And from far out here, each of them,
with their burning desires and insatiable thirsts
for all things they individually deem valuable,
resemble flies, blinking and flitting endlessly
until the end.

Process?

There's no secret,
no book that you can read,
no course or path that leads you to the answer,
it's all right there,
plain as your cherry lipstick,
but secret as the attitude behind your middle finger.
It's all time,
ticking seconds spent clicking away through the memories of a life
that has little to nothing to fight for,
but there's no secret to it;
it flows freely and falls out of the thumb pads.
I wish I could say that
there is a process;
sure, there is codification, imprisonment of the freedom of creation.
Yes, there's that, but there is nothing
else but time and thought.

Some people are simply luckier at doing things, maybe.

Whispers from Afar

I can hear you whispering,
telling me about the grey of the sky,
telling me that it's nowhere near the shade
when you cross the universe,
that here is so blue because the atmosphere
is set in its own way, and from that,
we derive that blue is clean and crisp and sharp,
something warm, and at the same time, so associated with
shivering or sweating glasses.

You're whispering that it's grey
that shows the coldest to us,
the true cold that blankets over the
top of every mood and leaves the metallic
aftertaste of a popsicle in your mouth.
I wish you weren't right about it.
I wish that you could be proven wrong, but
I know the tin foil taste too well;
I know the penny breath and the dime teeth,
how they clink and grind.

I want for there to be some greater color,
which I know there is,
but I want to be able to see past the spectrum of my own eyes,
down the uneven waves of light,
across the universe to you,
to view your purple thick sky
and your green sunsets
over oceans of liquid krypton,
so cold that the helium sky becomes thick as oxygen.

I'm not exactly envious;
I have my own world inside my head,
a world that stems from the roots of my own electronic,
irregular,
neurological impulses.
There, I'm so free;
There, I create objects devoid of meaning to others
but made of only meaning to me.

"for Conversation"

Bruise

Here we are sitting quiet, like we do.
We sit so quietly and breathe in the words that we don't say.
        "How'd you get this?"
I'm tracing the dark purple circle midway up your thigh.

"What?"
        "How?"
"Don't poke it; it hurts."
        "Sorry. Where did it come from?"
"From inside."

Your hands are so still, so old, and still, I never understood that.
How can we be young and still have these old parts of ourselves?
So knowledgeable your hands,
        "Inside?"
"I did it to myself."
        "Like a banana?"
"Yes."
        "But why?"
"It's cleaner than a cut."

You pad at it as if the blood were right there, waiting to find an es-
cape route. You breathe and I taste the words that you don't say,
wishing that senses were interchangeable.

        "No, I mean…why?"
"Just trying to wake up."

Benchmark

Sat down next to this man,
smoking, he was,
not me, I don't, can't, hate the taste,
tried it once when I was drunk.
I remember even through the falseness of alcohol
thinking that I didn't mix with this;
there he was though,
sucking the thin air through that white paper,
sat there "reading" my book,
watching the glowing red embers trace a line
straight into his mouth,
wondering if it got hotter the closer he drew it to him.

"Why do you smoke?" I asked.
     "Fuck you, kid, this is 2016."
"No, really though, what got you started?"

He blew out the contents of his lungs;
his teeth, I could see them, just right below his upper lip,
spoiled and sad, like teeth of someone that knows too much
and can't contain it.

I thought, knowledge rots you from the inside out.

He looked me up and up again,
     "Started smoking in 1971,
     when I was 13,
     they tasted better back then;
     now I just can't stop."

"Well, you know that it might kill you."

     "I hope so, kid, I hope so."

"and you and me"

"And you and me
and you and me, you said
and you and me."

He put his finger down in the pages,
creasing a line for the purpose of cessation,
letting the thought trail, feeling how thoughts
seem to become more liquid than liquid, spilling themselves
faster than one can explain, across the desert plains of the mind
and filling up marshes, causing the flowing of electric, moving rivers,
"How amazing is it," he thought,
"that the mind can move faster than the hands or the mouth?"

And the rushing river filled him up,
drowning him in the reiteration of "and you and me,"
for somehow something could be built on that,
something could be set upon the foundation of "and you and me"
because preceding it was possibility for action, or maybe just more.
Beyond it was possibility for action or maybe just silence and still,
maybe just the quiet of a sunset,
encapsulated between "me and you" and immortalized right before
the flash.

"People Don't Give a Shit About Poets"

"Why do you write that crap?"
        "What?"
"I said why do you–"
        "No, I heard you, I just don't get the question."

He had a joint pinched between his fingers,
sour, savory pot smoke wafting up through the gaps in his hand,
flew up through the old willow,
I can only imagine the bottom half
of the branches were stained the farther up you got;
he leaned in, kinda hunkered down on his haunches,
but somehow still fully reliant on the lawn chair.

"Like why do you even write all that shit man? People don't read
it."

He wasn't wrong.

        "I dunno."
"Exactly my point!
Why do something when you don't know why you're doing it?"
        "Ok, well why do you smoke that shit?"
"Because, man, we need to be able to escape from the world, find si-
lence in our minds, organize the stress
away."

        "And you think I don't do that with this?"

The sun had hit the edge of the world,
plummeting the east into a faded purple;
the west had a timbre of cowboys in silhouette
finding their telos at the end.
 "I guess, man, but you're wasting your time, people don't give a
shit about poets."

"Good thing I'm not doing it for them then."

Loss of Feelings

"Thanks, I quit."
      "Oh, so you don't…"
"Not since July 2014."

Funny his face, so twisted after the fact;
sadness usually followed by pity.
These, I recognize.

      "How'd you do it?"
"Medication. Doc got me some brain pills."
      "Did it hurt?"
"Nah, took some getting used to though."

Got used to finding the pattern of pills down the throat every day
for years.
      "Any side effects?"
"Sometimes a headache,
but a small price to pay for such a freedom."
      "Why'd you do it?"
"Just got sick of feeling so much all the time,
feeling everyone's feelings,
feeling my own heart too much,
feeling my life crumble while it was being built."
      "I see why you'd want to escape that."